Birthplace with Buried Stones

MEENA ALEXANDER

Birthplace with Buried Stones

Poems

TRIQUARTERLY BOOKS

NORTHWESTERN UNIVERSITY PRESS

EVANSTON, ILLINOIS

TriQuarterly Books
Northwestern University Press
www.nupress.northwestern.edu

Printed in the United States of America

10 9 8 7 6 5 4 3 2 1

Library of Congress Cataloging-in-Publication Data

Alexander, Meena, 1951–
 Birthplace with buried stones : poems / Meena Alexander.
  p. cm.
 Includes bibliographical references.
 ISBN 978-0-8101-5239-7 (pbk. : alk. paper)
 I. Title.
 PR9499.3.A46B55 2013
 811.54—dc23

                                                                    2013008694

For David

Contents

*

BIRTHPLACE WITH BURIED STONES

Experimental Geography

Everything about the railway station was erased, including the woman who was carrying a child with a patch of blood on his shirt.

I became all at once an American. This is a sentence very hard to translate.

One is singing. Two says: one flows.

You cannot know how things go. No Prophecy. Who can gainsay a bird singing in a suitcase?

She was seven and started praying as hard as she could. By her pillow moths flew, in the lemon tree a nest of honey bees grew.

An overdose of caravans caused her hair to fall out.

Our Father who art on earth—Lord of Sorrows and solar eruptions.

How many stars to hold the flag up? How many stripes to sink it? How many questions without answers?

Who becomes President if both he and the Vice President die?

The patch of blood on a child's shirt becomes a bird with no beak.

When the train arrived the refugees (for strictly speaking that is what they were) had no voice left in their throats.

Their clothing was quite dry. In spite of everything there was much singing.

I

KUBLAI: I do not know when you have had time to visit all the countries you describe to me. It seems to me you have never moved from this garden.

POLO: Everything I see and do assumes meaning in a mental space where the same calm reigns as here, the same penumbra, the same silence streaked by the rustling of leaves. At the moment when I concentrate and reflect, I find myself again, always, in this garden, at the hour of evening, in your august presence, though I continue, without a moment's pause, moving up a river green with crocodiles or counting the barrels of salted fish being lowered into the hold . . .

Perhaps this garden exists only in the shadow of our lowered eyelids . . .

—ITALO CALVINO, *INVISIBLE CITIES*

Morning Ritual

I sit in a patch of shade cast by a pipal tree.
Each morning I read a few lines from *The Narrow Road to the Deep North.*

Where did Bashō go?
He entered a cloud, and came out the other side:

Everything is broken and numinous.
Tiled roofs, outcrops of stone, flesh torn from mollusks.

Far away, a flotilla of boats. A child sucking stones.
There is a forked path to this moment.

Trees have no elsewhere.
Leaves very green.

Lychees

Terrace deep as the sky.
Stone bench where I sit and read,

I wandered by myself
Into the heart of the mountains of Yoshino.

In one hand a book, in the other, a bag made of newsprint—
No weather-beaten bones here

Just lychees bought in the market,
Thirty rupees per kilogram.

Stalks mottled red tied up with string,
Flesh the color of pigeon wings—

Sweet simmering.
Sunlight bruises air

Pine trees blacken.
Where shall I go?

The Dhauladhar peaks
Are covered in snow.

Red Bird

These lines are for a child who counts out potatoes
And hands them to his mother,

She rinses them in the village stream—
Freckled red of potato skins, the color of the bird

Whose name is marked in long inscriptions, in copper plate
In a kingdom south of the mountains.

BRYANT PARK

Striped umbrellas lift in the breeze:
Two girls, one in a red shift dress, the other in white.

The one in lacy white has tight hair,
She spreads a fan with her fingers.

The fan is painted with swans and catalpa leaves.
The swans have lifted beaks.

I think she was part of Bashō's snow-viewing party.
I'd like to sit in Bryant Park in midwinter, and catch the snow,

Skaters too, looping on ice, lolling gestures of the man
Who proposes to sing a song with my name in it,

Five dollars flat, recession rate.
A woman called Butterfly gave Bashō a piece of white silk to write on.

It helped him a lot.
I think she had fish-shaped eyes, like the girl in the scarlet dress.

You are far away as the mountains of Yoshino.
Give me your hand, maybe then I can write a poem.

I want to add: I cannot live without you
But I am doing it anyhow.

Near Sendai

Butterfly blown
Into a mountain hole,
Wild iris cradled in darkness.

Cover your nose and mouth if you can
With bits of old cloth, drink iodine too—
Children bright and burning.

Let your shadow lead you.
Carve this line into cold rock
In memory of the place where Bashō walked.

Bamboo

I stroll in a bamboo grove,
Birds pepper colored cling to the branches.

By the tomb of Sikandar Lodi
Your shadow comes to me—

A man in a lungi
Who is starving himself very slowly.

Blood, spittle, sandalwood, phlegm
What the body expels—

Flesh has a scent,
You beside me, forever (lost).

Suite 19, Viceregal Lodge

In my room a screen,
Pale silk in tatters,

I undress in the light of the mountains.
On the terrace monkeys dance.

One keeps a mirror in its claws
Another a burning orb

A third has its face blacked out:
On its head a cap with a snarl of blue

You once gave me.
Monkeys gnaw buds, topple flowerpots.

Stand in the way of the flowering jasmine
I hear you whisper

That way I can smell you
Even when I'm gone.

Landscape with Ghost

Two glasses, one chipped, a bowl with a crust of salt,
A bitter flash in air—

Lord Curzon's daughter whispers in the deodar leaves,
Unravels her hair.

Monkeys dart through clouds, they are long tailed and bear no malice,
Some are winged like cherubim.

She loiters in the corridor where princes were forced to stand,
She refuses food and drink.

Where is the lover she met at Scandal Point?
Below them, wild horses galloped, manes flaring.

Dear Diary,
I do not know who he is anymore.

I do not like your hands.
They are too foreign.

She needs Hanuman with his herb of healing
But the clouds won't part.

On a rocky path where squirrels leapt,
She creeps past a mass of dead bees

To reach a mound littered with cut hair,
Plastic bottles, filaments of ash.

In the gorge below,
Two women raise firewood in their arms.

Smoke rises
From a fiery tulasi plant.

Lady Dufferin's Terrace

In the old Viceregal lodge silk paisley and damask on the walls,
Rosewood staircase skittish on damp rock.

Rajahs stopped to water their horses, British armies dithered in heat,
Cattle crept uphill.

On unequal ground the shadow of wings—
Restless calligraphy.

Afternoons I go downhill in search of bottled water
And Britannia biscuits.

When I was a child ayah gave me biscuits to dip in tea
In a house with a mango grove not far from the sea.

Beauty swallows us whole.
I try to imagine your face without stubble on it.

In Boileauganj market I step into a pothole—
It's filled with shining water,

Desire makes ghosts of us.
Earthworms glisten in papaya peel.

Merchants squat in wooden shops
Hawking hair oil and liver pills.

A lorry with a blue god rattles past.
Krishna's right hand

Is stretched in benediction.
His eye, bruised.

Come twilight I sip cold water,
Stretch out on a chaise longue,

I am distracted by monkeys
Clawing stone pineapples on Lady Dufferin's terrace.

A cloud floats down, covering us all.
I turn on an oil lamp and write to you:

Dear X—Where are you now?
In the mess on Observatory Hill

They serve us rice, dal, and sliced onions.
Also green chilis, the color of parrot wings.

Lady Dufferin Writes to Her Mother

I ride along the edge of a precipice holding up a parasol.
—LADY DUFFERIN, SHIMLA, 1886

Miss Gough was a white cat complete with claws,
And Lord William, a Chelsea Pensioner hobbling along.

Mr. Rosen, beard dyed black did his Afghanish walk
With a lady in a sack—on her eyes, a bit of net to see through.

Children stuck noses against glass—
They saw me in orange, a Sheridan picture,

Stiff bustle, starch in my hair.
Did they think I was a Himalayan cockatoo?

He comes to me in dreams, Queen Victoria's munshi,
Little Indian chap who serves her well—

Why waste your time taking tea with a woman
Who dresses up as a white cat?

He was speaking of Miss Gough at our Fancy Dress Ball,
The one we had in the Viceregal lodge last week.

—Think of our poet who nibbled salt of the conquerors
And suffered so when you lot sacked Delhi—

He muttered the name Ghalib, adding something
About souls of the dead poking out of dirt as tulips do.

That night I slept badly.
At dawn I got the maid to make my water very hot,

I slipped into the tub with the golden claws.
In the garden a poplar swayed in the breeze,

A boy thrust his goats up rock.
Poor child, his head streaked with filth.

At our ball, Mrs. Bliss was the White Lady of Avenel,
Hair flowing over silks to the polished floor.

I never saw such hair before, as if the setting sun
Had crept into her skull and burnt it.

Now the munshi whispers in my ear—
See how blood glows in the Beloved's cheek!

Dear Mama—Where is Killyleagh Castle,
Where Clandeboye now?

Worlds swarm in me.
Soon we'll be spirits in this land we've come to.

Mountains hang under clouds,
And a light I cannot name wells up from the ground.

II

The Territory Argent – that never yet – consumed –

—EMILY DICKINSON

June Air

All summer I wanted to hold tight
To what I felt was the truth—

A penurious thing.
All I had was our breath, an unsteady pulsing

·With holes enough
For a swallow to fly through.

I remember one in our room
Hovering by the portrait of someone else's ancestors,

A girl skirts askew, eyes half shut,
Seated on a tricycle.

Behind her, hands cradling her shoulders,
A boy bruised by paint.

The bird swam by the gilt ceiling
Then startled, dashed itself against the window frame.

After the beating wings were done
Hills clarified in darkness.

Bits of light fell from the sky.
We watched not knowing what it all was,

The air hurting us into happiness
We never really thought was possible.

Sun, Stone

From a hot stone
A grasshopper dropped

Into your palm,
You held a green heart, beating.

This bitten cliff is *calanque*—
The word in Provençal

Comes from *kal,*
Stone in your mother tongue.

The same sun strikes us
Here as in your childhood,

No elsewhere.
A man is casting off in a boat.

High above
A woman clings to a tree,

Her wild skirts blowing.
She cannot see him

So she imagines
The man with trousers

Rolled up,
Stepping into a boat

With a single
Transparent sail.

The figures on the wharf
Grow tiny.

No one knows quite how
They sang in Provençal,

Or how on the *calanque*
In the green wings

Of her skirt
The love notes rang.

In the Garden of Freemasons

Gnats flee into thickets
Swans too, in search of periodic water.

I brood on Jibanananda Das, poems tucked
Into a notebook, returning from the book fair,

Struck dead by a tramcar, aged fifty-four.
On tendrils of dirt, in the spot where he fell

Spirits cluster. Children sing to each other
Tossing balls as children do,

A mechanical bird tethered with wire
Circles a stall of neon-colored bras, panties too.

Needing a place to wait for you
(Chowringhee undid me)

I sit on a flat stone in the garden of Freemasons.
What did the poet say about swans, nine of them, mystical?

He did not know why there were nine
Vanishing into trees, but that there were nine

He was sure.
It's dark in your city, clouds cover the moon,

The House of Freemasons tilts
With the weight of gnats' wings.

Under a crystal chandelier,
When he's sure no one is looking,

A man with red hair polishes his own shoes.
Don't go away, think of the poem

I hear you say—
It's all you need to do now, or ever really.

Landscape with Kurinji Flowers

A forked road leads to no season that I know,
Footpath dusty, sideways drifting into a coil of bushes
Pistils milk-mad, mouthing—

Love one another or die.
Feverish imaginings surely, trying to figure out where on earth we are,
Here in the only place we have.

Time's lapse, a torn shutter,
A click hoisting us into a landscape
Flicked by clouds, a blaze, a scattering,

Harvest scored by bees.
The ether of longing dragged in my mouth
And in your mouth, the taste of mine, utterly secret.

We are made up of place—
Corpuscles of soil, reamed with chalcedony
Dirt of broken blood vessels, cliffs scarred with bloodstone,

Gobs of gunfire, grenades' catarrh,
Red runnels of water, an offering to the gods
Who barely speak to us anymore.

Years from now, where will we be?
Sitting in sunlight on warm stones at the edge of a wall?
Pacing a hospital floor

As the wounded are brought in?
Or, in some terrible dream of home, rinsed clean, sky-blown
Shot free of a stumbling story?

Damage

I. Moonlight

Seeing you, I could not shut my eyes.
It would be true to say I did not get one hour of sleep.

Through the window, thickets of snow,
A placket of plane trees,

Someone else's tomb—
Whose I do not know.

The moon near full slips out of its petticoat,
Swims through window glass.

What's between us: fierce, moist, rumpled
Like these bedclothes, shimmering in body heat.

II. Dream Time

In a waking dream, I press my palm
To the slope of your face,

Touch you where hair sprouts,
Blunt mouth hair—regardless.

I have grown to love you against my will.
I say this as if the will

Counted
In this sort of thing.

III. Future Perfect

The horoscope is exact—
It says you and I

Will step down
Into darkness together.

This was based
On matching sun signs.

The spotted hawk
Drops from the moon.

No one sees it.

IV. Underground

A woman in the subway,
In a fawn colored skirt,

Grips a bright cello
Between her knees.

Scarlet, not the cello itself
Rather, its case.

The tunnel is something else.
We cannot know it

Except as aftermath—
Sempiternal rack, love's toil.

After the burning
Strings of the cello reverberate,

So too your breath:
A slight hiss, a quiver.

V. Future Imperfect

Lacking you, I am spat
Out of the god's mouth

Together with red spittle,
Betel nut juice,

Flesh and bones.
Altogether voided, without you.

When I am alone
The god presses hard

On my throat.
He is angry, clairvoyant.

VI. Damage

In my mind
You stroke my shoulder bone

Through voile.
How can the body

Exist in the mind
Like that—you and I touching?

I used to dress in voile petticoats
When I was a child.

Now a blouse,
A summer's usage, merely.

Our bodies are filled with bone.
Surely you know that?

You see it with accidents
Of all sorts—

Some deliberate
Others not.

The wounded one
Lying on the sidewalk,

In between parked cars,
Flowering trees

With umber petals,
Bones terribly displayed.

VII. Cell Phone

I call you—it's twilight,
The street fills with birds

Hundreds of them, sparrows, starlings
Wings whirling, claws raised,

Tiny flying machines.
Their cries crowd the air

Drown out my voice.
What gods drew them here

Out of the groves
Of oak and ash?

Why don't they swarm
To the mountaintop

Where the gods live?
Why don't they leave us alone?

VIII. Sweet Dark

Press me to your ribs,
Cup my left breast with its freckle,

Set your right hand to my throat.
The monsoon's in our room,

Doors swollen, shutters blown.
Rampant, your flesh.

Singing starts—
The gods are returning

From long exile,
From a stony mountaintop

They long for the sweet dark
We will give it to them.

IX. Ghosts

The painted body covering the bare body
Belongs to the self on stage—

This is written in the *Nātyaśāstra.*
Let the painted hand carry a fan

Scented with sandalwood and attar,
Let the bare hand carry a phantom fan.

When the lover approaches
The lacquered fan will cool the painted body,

And the fan in the naked hand
Shall set a ghostly self on fire.

Cantata for a Riderless Horse

I

A child sees a man on a flying trapeze,
Face swathed in pink tulle, bomb tucked to his belly.

Behind him, a car squares off in air,
Wheels lambent, turning.

In the bleakness of space, everything is still.
The bomb lands in a pile of straw dragged from the stables.

The circus tent glows,
The fire is insuperable, seemingly without cause,

The bomb a misshapen egg hurts no one,
The tent in flames

Is a nothing but a rag and bone shop,
Sty of memory.

II

We like to think of the inner life
As the cause of things.

One might as well say that the happiness
Of Sanskrit is the cause of speech

As Novalis did when he was very young.
Was he watching death round the corner,

Past the broken barn on the mountainside
With the tangle of blue flowers no one else noticed?

Death in the shape of an old horse
Tied to a laurel tree,

Acid in its nostrils, still snorting.
The stables I saw in my dreams

(Source of the straw that cradled the bomb)
Are filled with anxious horses.

III

In the Ashwamedha rite, a white horse let loose
Roams through territory war must claim.

The horse is sacrificed and a great queen,
I think of Draupadi here,

Lies down beside the smoking parts.
In Pune, when I was a child

We lived on Ganeshkind Road.
In the wedding season

I saw a pale horse bearing a bridegroom,
His face veiled in flowers.

I willed her to sit beside him
Clutching the horse's flanks,

A bride, sari storm red,
Slashed with gold.

On the garden line, on the white sheet amma hung
In midsummer before the rains came,

Male and female turned to shadows,
Mixing with the horse's flesh.

IV

I had no chiseled gold to bring,
You had no horse, no drums.

All we had was a dusty town, a mountaintop,
Wild flowers, ceaseless mist.

I married you in the midst of what I felt
Was a war in my own life.

But who the parties were I could not say,
Even if forced to the edge of a cliff.

The war continued,
But now you were a party to it.

In the midst of this we had our children.
With what lay to hand—

A scrap of paper, a ream of string
We made a shelter of straw

With a wishbone in it.
The bleached bone snapped.

The young ones turned
Into precious hostages.

We bought a house in the woods,
A stalwart thing of wood and brick:

When dinner plates chipped,
Or a squirrel dropped down the chimney

A black walnut clutched in its claws,
When deer ravaged the blue spruce

Or bullfinches sucked up earthworms
At the edge of a pond

Where our children swam
Mud splayed on their thighs,

I glimpsed the desolation
Of earthly paradise.

V

Reared on betrayal
I could not bear to be happy.

I flinched at truth
Buried in muscle and skin,

Intricate loops of blood—
Mute harrowing.

Survival of the fittest parts of the self
I thought was what was called for.

Like a woman who wears a wig
To conceal stubble on the skull,

I coveted the split ends
Of desire.

Hurt poured into our hands.
When I touched her, I flinched—

A child clinging to a horse,
Pink suit shimmering with sweat,

Eyes clammed tight
Willing the man on the flying trapeze to drop,

Willing the bomb to splinter his ribs
Into fractions of glass,

The tent etched in rainbow colors,
Smeared with ash.

VI

There is something desolate in us
That tries to lay love waste.

But love too has its daring,
Its unbegotten species of sense making.

I come to you now,
Dirt in my hair

From a country road
Where we saw a white horse

Rear its hooves.
A helicopter rattled by.

Was it spraying crops?
Who could tell?

Shall we sing to her, the child hidden in a cloud?
Who knows if we can wake her.

Coda

Yesterday, I folded up our clothes. It seemed to me they smelt of wild grass
From the edge of the mountain where we lay, rocks streaked indigo,

Accidental hue of a scarf you bought me a century ago
On a street where men strolled, mirrors strapped to their backs,

Crying out in words I learn to understand—*Move away, danger!*
Somehow the mirrors held in the crush of rickshaws, cows, camels,

Caravanserai of women, palms marked with the shapes of mango leaf and moon,
Bitter blossoms. As you nudged me on

I saw smoke from a tent, a riderless horse without saddle or tinsel,
Only reins on its throat, led forward by a child whose face we could not see.

(For D. S. L.)

Mother, Windblown

Je cherche la chanson, je dois la retrouver...
—MARIE ETIENNE

I. Housekeeper

Why such wandering—
What has happened to home?

The ruinous everyday,
How to cope with that?

To have given birth once, twice,
And before that, to have borne witness

To a clot of blood
Drained into a china bowl.

It was up there in the mountains,
Where we loved each other,

Close to a forest of whistling deodar,
Deer too, ears pricked up.

II. Metal Mirror

To turn,
As if memory were a mirror (how trite it sounds).

But birds are pecking the air
Inside out,

A squall of pigeons and parrots
On loose stones,

Hammer-toed quail, and horsemen
Desperate for conquest

Racing past women threshing millet
In the city of Iltutmish, in the year 1230.

Then and now
Markets crashed, painted birds flung back.

III. Interlingual

No, not that deaf, grave past,
Rather to be here where I have gone on

Saying yes, yes—always yes!
To reel backwards,

To be gathered (as the vagina bleeds)
Into unerring lightness.

Later, the mottled part,
The hair speckled part

Bejeweled and puffed up,
(Who made these colors?)

Translated
Into a mother tongue

Which no one can hear
For very long.

IV. Himalaya

Once a seven-week creature
Paddling inside, scraped out.

Twice, a nine-month creature
Thrust out, wailing.

Boy and girl, sticky and sweet
All sucking mouth and shit.

Later we were mother
And two children who had no boat

To cross the dark river,
Ferocious fastness

Wind pleated
At the foot of the mountain.

V. There Is No Subject

It still hurts inside,
Light pulled up out of me

And a great light pressing down.
I don't know how else to put it,

Ribs thrust open,
The future impenitent.

Who will teach you patience
Scarlet sash

Culpable in beauty,
O extravagant umbilicus

Empress of all festivals?
In the mirror (needful now)

A doe shorn.
Quivering flesh,

Her work done.
Or not, not ever.

Coda (Sky-Water)

Borne north in dreams
There are lights in the sky, driven lights.

I swim freely
(Ponder the adverb)

Through a ring of gold
Encircling a boat,

Timbers splintered,
Winged boat

Found in the Jardin des Vestiges,
What the Phoenicians fled

As death came calling.
On a cloudy slope

Deer nibble cut stalks
Of deodar and chir pine.

Syllables tumble
In a milky river:

Babbling mother
Font of memory.

Boy from Rum

A lad from Rum
Is lost in a garden of creatures
Who have no tongue.

They make music brushing wings,
Fleshly things that pour down the back,
All muscle and grit.

He stumbles through a mess of shrubs,
Comes upon a girl seated in a pavilion.
Her face is cut in gold.

Under her flows a channel of milk.
My son comes with singing words
From the duc d'Orléans who lived

In the same time as the boy from Rum
(Struck dumb in a garden painted
For a Muslim emperor, king of kings).

My son who is tall and lean like
The lad from Rum, dressed though
In jeans and black wool jacket,

Plucks off his cap and sings
Quand je fus pris au pavillon,
Je me brûlay à la chandelle, ainsi que fait le papillon.

He sips warm milk, nibbles at bruised
Cookies I have made for him.
Restless then, he plucks up the phone, and sings.

Does she hear,
An old woman, his mother's mother
Stooped at the edge of a veranda

Where monsoon mists pour?
It's night time there.
Someone sets a candle at her side.

No words only music:
This is my whole dream.
Dull witted moths spill into flame.

Nocturnal with Ghostly Landscape on St. Lucy's Day

I

Morning on St. Lucy's Day,
Mist at the mouth of a tea plantation

Where a pagoda was built, someone's dream of China
In hills where orchids cling to banyan roots

Whose twisting roots surrender
To ghosts risen from fields of dark water.

A boy comes to his mother, white rose in hand,
Makes as if to give it to her.

But she skips to sounds of an invisible flute,
Notes that strike rocks by the useless pagoda of the grandparents,

Her eyes shut, skirts drawn up and teacup
Filled with emptiness. Abruptly he reaches out,

Then draws back, a push-pull thing, fist with paper cone,
Masking an exquisite bloom.

II

In a waking dream the mother hears her boy
Slam the door, stride into the street.

He stumbles into a pothole packed with shards of bone,
Burnt exhaust pipes, stained Kevlar vests.

He lies there as another lad, with sharp elbows like her boy's,
But with dripping sandy hair,

Floats up from the Tigris River,
Unhooks his phantom leg.

The wound fills the TV screen,
Crimson halo dissolving this chaos of derivatives:

Houses foreclosed, stocks tumbling,
A candidate who cries out for Eden,

His slender brown hands
Taut, clasped to the arcana of the everyday—

That which is all around and will not let us be.
Also the horror of what we have done

Or let be done in our lifetime, a small difference there,
Necessary for a self to survive more or less sane.

III

It's late on St. Lucy's Day, darkness pours.
Incarnadine the kitchen knife,

The tuning fork of despair.
A mother reaches for the windowpane,

Searching for her son.
Clouds soar, she spots the moon,

Spun discus glittering on the Hudson River,
The swamps of Shatt al Arab,

A painted pagoda in a lost plantation,
The curtain of childhood dropping

As St. Lucy turns, her throat a column of tears,
Part of our planet's luminous geography:

Still clothed in savage reeds,
She raises her eyes on a platter.

(In memory of Grace Paley, 1922–2007)

Jerusalem Poems

Teatro Olimpico

At three in the afternoon,
A girl tumbling out of an unmade bed—

Skirts juniper colored, she rushes out of the room
Sand in between her toes and in the creases of her knees.

She runs very fast
Towards what was once a prison yard.

She stops in a clump of rosebush and thorn
Strips off her coat.

Through a hole in a brick wall
She leaps onto the stage Palladio made.

Above her, a ceiling where clouds drift.
Is that a ghostly horseman?

Clouds sift a future that gods painted
In scarlet and gold can scarcely comprehend.

Why search for the seven roads of Thebes?
There are fresh tragedies waiting for her.

A bitter wall of concrete cuts the sky,
In its shadow a woman kneels.

Eyes shut tight she sings
To a lad laid in the dirt,

Bullet holes in his hands and feet.
In his wounds wild roses bloom.

Nocturne

We have come to Haifa where the sea starts.
The theater Al-Midani floats by a tree.
I see this clearly though a dark filament twists round the moon.
I tiptoe through surf—
A rope someone left at the end of the jetty,
I knot it to my ankle,
Not wanting to be swept away by sudden longing.
Inside the theater, candles, a mountain of bloom.
Does Haifa have almond blossom?
Must they gather it from the edges of the sea?
Someone was shot point-blank and killed—
A man who kept waiting for the good life to occur,
For the mouth to speak what comes before speech,
Sap in the tree and firmament of flesh.

A child approaches me in the darkened theater
And whispers in my ear—Yes we are waiting for Godot—
I am overcome by the scent of tuberoses
And cigarette smoke and can't reply—
Yes, many friends of the dead man are smoking.
Six or seven take turns reading from a poem.
They pass the pages from hand to hand—
I left my gloom hanging on a branch of boxthorn
And the place weighed less.
A woman in black jeans forces open the windows.
The moon uncorks herself and blows away.
So this is how the sea starts: increments of longing,
Mostly in half darkness
Then a white light as waves rush through.

Cobblestones and Heels

By Herod's Gate,
In a twelfth-century courtyard,

A woman in sweatpants,
Nails flashing crimson.

By her, a parrot in a cage.
—Tu tu tu tu hutu tu—the parrot cries.

By the cage stones shift.
See this foot? She lifts up her heel.

1967, they napalmed us.
Imagine that, stones where a saint knelt,

Pitted by fire.
Baba Farid, you know him, yes?

We buried grandmother in her dress of flame.
I keep her chain, always

She pointed a foot—
Gold swirled over torn bone.

On the ankle, under a loop of gold,
Savage indentation.

She fastened the stiletto shoe,
Steadied herself

Against a parrot's cage.
Hutu tu—tututu—I hear it moan

Shadow hopping on a heap of stone.

I wear heels now—
Take pride in my flesh,

Display what cuts.

We are strangers to this life
I and you.

Using a white hanky
She veils her face

Then rips it off, goes on talking.
We see signs, that's all—

A dragonfly on a heap of green almonds,
Right by Damascus Gate,

Water in our taps
Turning the color of burnt salt,

By the leaking gas station
On the road to Abu Dis

Spray painted on the separation wall,
Huge letters—

Boys do it
When darkness falls—

Love sees no Color.
Dirt whispers, I'm coming home.

Indian Hospice

Yesterday, it rained so hard
Lemons spilt from the lemon tree
And rolled over cobblestones in my Jerusalem courtyard.

I thought of Baba Farid
Who came on a pilgrimage centuries ago.
In a hole cut from rock by the room where I sleep,

He stood for forty days and nights
Without food or drink. Nothing for him was strange
In the way his body slipped into a hole in the ground,

And nothing was not.
Rust in the stones and blood at the rim of his tongue.
In the humming dark

He heard bird beaks stitching webs of dew,
Sharp hiss of breath let out from a throat,
Whose throat he did not know.

Was it his mother crying O Farid, where are you now?
It's what she did when he swung
Up and down, knees in a mango tree,

Head in the mouth of a well,
Singing praises to God.
Crawling out of his hole, welts on his cheeks,

And underfoot in bedrock—visionary recalcitrance.
A lemon tree wobbled in a high wind.
Under it, glistening in its own musk, the black iris of Abu Dis.

Wild with the scents of iris and lemon he sang—O Farid
This world is a muddy garden,
Stone, fruit, and flesh all flaming with love.

Garden in Nazareth

Already birds are flying into your garden,
Lark and quail, sand in their wings.

The garden is in front, the desert is not far.
Somewhere a bus is burning.

Your wife enters, tray in hand—heaped with fennel shining,
Cut apples, loquats, pears.

Sweet and cooked scents rise in your sickroom,
Man-mountain sitting up in bed,

On your head a cap of wool, a blue stripe on it.
You balance a thimbleful of coffee in your hand.

I stare at your furrowed palm, fit to clutch pen or spade,
Dig for memory.

How long have you been in this garden?
Twenty million years! Your voice is hoarse—

A stream under red rocks.
I think of Saffuriyya, your village destroyed,

I think of a girl with auburn hair, where is she now?
Do you know the Panchatantra,

The hare and the tortoise story?
We are like that, the tortoise in the dry land.

It lives in our head.
You look to the side, fall quiet.

A tear rolls from your eye.
I cannot bear it now and say—Taha Muhammad Ali, sir,

Your poems are a garden. The sky is beyond us.
The garden will outlast us.

You seem not to hear.
You slip against the pillow, push yourself up again.

I lean forward, adjust the blanket.
The birds, I say, there are many birds in your garden.

Your face lights up. Sunlight on your face.
A thread of gold breaks the sky.

You stretch out a hand
Reaching for a world we have not seen,

A life of sound and circling sense
Vivid air, the wound of mist,

Perpetual benediction:
A woman boils milk, on an old stove,

Pours it into a metal cup,
Hands it to a man just back from the fields.

A boy cradles a quivering mouse in his hands,
He's rescued it from a trap.

A girl with auburn hair,
Dressed in checked skirt and white blouse

Plucks apricots by a stream.
Overhead clouds part.

Close at hand, beside a mound of sand
A broken comb, a burning bush:

An old, old story—the bush burns
And is not consumed,

The leaves are scarlet,
The leaves are filled with singing syllables.

(In memory of Taha Muhammad Ali, 1931–2011)

Impossible Grace

At Herod's Gate
I heap flowers in a crate

Poppies, moist lilies—
It's dusk, I wait.

*

Wild iris—
The color of your eyes before you were born

That hard winter
And your mother brought you to Damascus Gate.

*

My desire silent as a cloud,
It floats through New Gate

Over the fists
Of the beardless boy-soldiers.

*

You stopped for me at Lion's Gate,
Feet wet with dew

From the torn flagstones
Of Jerusalem.

*

Love, I was forced to approach you
Through Dung Gate

My hands the color
Of the broken houses of Silwan.

*

At Zion's Gate I knelt and wept.
An old man, half lame—

He kept house in Raimon's café,
Led me to the fountain.

*

At Golden Gate,
Where rooftops ring with music,

I glimpse your face.
You have a coat of many colors—impossible grace.

Mamilla Cemetery

The nymph of the wept-for fountain . . .
—RILKE

I

She waits for me under a green almond tree
Right in the middle of the cemetery,

In front of a broken stone marking a man's death.
Glyphs dissolve—her voice clarifies:

Why are you here in Ma'man Allah Cemetery?
You should have stayed in the marketplace in Nablus,

With mounds of sweet konafa
Gleaming vessels filled with tea,

Or stopped with the children playing ball
And flying kites of bristling paper

Right by the separation wall—
Bare-legged children, wind in their hair.

You could have sat in Bethlehem
With women sewing bits of cloth,

Threads iridescent, like sunbirds' wings.
Why come to this nest of lamentations?

II

I come I said for love alone
—Though I barely know what this might mean—

And because I heard you calling me.
Black hair blown back over her face,

Hair stung with flecks of golden chamomile,
I watched her gaze at me.

Her eyes bloodshot, soot under her lids,
And all about on dusty ground

Dropped from the almond tree, half-moons of green
Torn and pecked by passing crows.

Her voice surprised me though, low,
Resolute even.

III

What is it you want to know?
She rose, swirling her skirts:

Stuck to the gleaming silk
Hundreds of shards

They looked like crawling silkworms,
Maggots even, sucked from earth.

Don't be scared, come closer now:
After the bulldozers,

After the men with cardboard boxes,
I kneel in wet grass,

In between the torn gravestones
And the ones defaced with paint

I gather what I can.
She held up her wrists, bruised,

Dark as a sparrow's wing.
I have work to do.

Each night
I wash my hands in moonlight

Then gather up these precious bones.
Bit by bit I polish them

Using my hands and hair,
Using smooth stones.

I breathe on these ancestral bones
Until they glow

Winged things, they soar into a wheel of stars
High above Jerusalem.

IV

Yes, I admit my life is odd.
I sleep in that tree,

The one with black flowers.
It blooms by the gate you came through,

Easiest that way,
No rent to pay, no landlord to trouble me.

Don't you agree?
Then something took hold of her.

The creak perhaps of a lorry at the gate
Or was it the mewl of a cat from the parking lot

Paved over the unquiet dead?
She wiped her face with the back of her hand,

Settled her skirts
—O incandescent burden—

One hand gripping a green branch
She leant against the almond tree.

V

Her words were notes struck on a painted oud,
An abyss broke between us:

When you stand in monsoon rain,
Remember me—

The child of Lamentation
And sister of Memory,

Youngest of the muses,
The one who whistles in the wind at dawn,

Who kneels by the clogged stream
To open the fountain of joy:

I am a creature of water and salt,
Of bitter herbs and honey—

A torn sail on the river Jordan,
I long to be free.

April 16, 2011, Nablus–December 26, 2011, Tiruvella

House of Clouds

Clouds float over Giudecca Island,
Over a renovated factory, marked *Hotel Stucky.*

In the house of clouds
Voices of children torn from their mothers.

One cries, Go west to catch the sun!
East by the isthmus it grows darker.

Go find the almond tree
That grows in the ghetto,

By the café without walls.
There you'll find see my shadow.

I am Isaac,
The boy with the torn knee.

Tintoretto saw me
Squatting on a stone

A knife
Above my neck bone.

Once I danced
In fields of red anemone

At the foot of Mount Moriah.
Remember me.

Song for Isaac

Isaac, you are falling—
I am too.

Neither cotton
Nor silk

To cover the hole,
A ram's horn

Jutting
Through blue.

Who lives there?
We thought God knew.

With short steps
I have made

A long journey
To elsewhere,

Isaac.

III

I'm carried in my shadow
like a violin
in its black case.

—TOMAS TRANSTRÖMER

La Prima Volta

A small girl trying to read the leaves
This is how I began:

Fleshly syllables pressed
Against mango bark,

Owls in the topmost branches
Nodding before the storm slashed.

I try to understand the desperate quiet
Of beings—

Father, Child, Holy Ghost,
Self-same host, torn lotus bloom,

Four-footed ox loitering,
Heavier than heaven

When meaning starts.
In wet grass, the winnowing.

Autobiography

Out of a porthole a child pokes her head.
Rocks prance under water,

Sunlight burns a hole in air
Fit for a house to fall through.

Palm trees dive into indigo.
Where is Kochi now?

Out on deck men raise glasses of cognac,
Women in chiffon saris

Giggle at the atrocious accents of the poor
Trapped in the holds with their tiny cooking stoves

And hunks of burlap to sleep in.
Between sari hems and polished toes,

The child sees flying fish
Vomited by the sea—

Syllables lashed to their rainbow wings,
Tiny bodies twisting in heaps.

Sea salt clings to them.
The sea has no custom, no ceremony.

It makes a theater for poetry,
For a voice that splits into two, three:

Drunken migrations of the soul.
No compass to the sea. The sea is memory.

Water Crossing

I

I was born into a house where music didn't matter,
But now I know it is the one thing that counted—

An earthly music scraped from root and rock.
Stones stirred when no one was looking,

The house with its courtyard started to float.
Limestone quickened into fists and thighbones,

Handprints flowered on bedroom walls
Thumbs cut off, ancient marks of mutilation,

Wrists the color of glaciers before they split
And water poured into the open fields.

Then came the scents of wild lavender
Flung from the other side of the globe,

Thickets of it, sprung here and there
Making a rare sound—a single note torn open

And lengthened, as far as it would go—
A violet sound no one could have missed,

Even at sunset as far west as we were going
Up the Red Sea with its blunt sandstone cliffs.

II

When I turned five, high wind and water
Swallowed what I could remember:

A mango grove where beetles danced,
Symmetries of silk, saris of mild cotton

Grandmother's blackened pearls and so much more.
Amma was with me but I was all alone,

We had each other but our life was lost.
Salt water curved its sonorous being

To what the eye could bear in weight of loneliness.
Was this what it was to live in the world?

Time turned transparent. Pentimento of pastoral—
I had to teach myself much later and with inordinate effort.

We set foot on sand, I held tight to her hand.
Amma and I saw dry trees heave,

Guns on the cliffs started to stutter.
It was a tongue we had not heard before.

Waves clustered, rose into a fountain.
But what can music do against the weapons of soldiers?

Summer Splendor

She rides in an acre of sand, past half-baked houses,
Quarter notes of despair, a desert music.

Ahead, a river dark and shining.
She props her bicycle against a ficus tree.

Tied with a rope, a boat with Coca-Cola crates,
Metal rods, broken statuary.

Can she slip into the fishy stench,
Budding breasts, pubic hair, hot heart stammering?

Embrace a figure wrapped in cloth,
Ibis-headed god

Brilliant eye and turquoise beak—
He who unlocks speech, pours out prophetic song?

Dreary, squatting in the reeds,
Singing back to the god, she dreams herself free.

The bird quavering in the ficus tree
Could not do more.

When she straightens up,
Mud on her skirt, a fetching thing, polka dots in black and jade

Stitched by a tailor on Kasr Avenue.
She stops by a silver sign—*Khartoum Station*—

Glimpsing Gordon Pasha's headless ghost
Throat simmering in sunlight.

In a whitewashed house
By a mirror propped on a tin trunk, her mother waits.

Over the trunk a throw of Belgian lace—
She smooths the folds of her sari,

Stiff cotton set loose by circling air,
Then turns, transfixed by impromptu sounds.

A summer splendor:
Crickets, whirring fruit flies, sand grouse in heat,

And streaming into the mirror—
Someone else's eyes filled with blank misgivings.

Migrant Memory

I

I try to remember a desert town,
Mirages at noon, at dusk a dusty lawn

Bottles of gin and scotch, a mathematician
To whom I spoke of reading Proust all summer long.

His mistress stood on tiptoe wiping his brow with her pent up silk,
Her sari, hot green rivaling the neem leaves.

Watching her, amma whispered in the wind—Be real.
Take a husband of good stock. As for love, it's blind.

Appa's voice low—No dowry. You're all you need,
Your own precious self.

II

A lifetime ago grandmother Eli wore gold,
Stepped off a boat into a paddy field and vanished.

Ink inches forward in her diary.
Place absolves us, distances startle,

Turmeric pounded on stone, crushed fenugreek
She kept in a jar by her bedside. Why, no one knew.

When the neem starts to flower, we'll use the petals for chutney.
Gandhi is coming out of jail soon.

Two rupees for a new teapot, we need it badly.
Three for a sack of sugar.

Fear humps in me—a pregnancy.
Who will do the embroidery on my little one's skirt?

III

Canyons of dirt crop up in a tree-lined garden
Doorways slide into rubble.

Where is grandmother now?
I need a golden ratio for loss.

Can Fibonacci's theorem ease the hazard of memory?
Under cloud cover I enter Combray.

Proust approaches wrapped in a Fortuny robe:
On his knobbly knees

Two peacocks woven in silk
Sip from a vase set in a field emblazoned

With syllables of Sanskrit.
She leans against his shoulder, my grandmother,

The nationalist who has burnt her silks.
She wears finest khadi draped about her heels.

She follows him into his cork-lined room.
He finds a dry twig, sets it in a glass.

Years pass.
Shreds of green surround the central aureole,

Shocking pink.
A haboob blows, shutters explode—

Grandmother's gold, sunk in time's flood,
And in the dusty capital

Where I spent my early years,
A boy soldier bathed in his own blood.

For My Father, Karachi 1947

Mid-May, centipedes looped over netting at the well's mouth.
Girls grew frisky in summer frocks, lilies spotted with blood.

You were bound to meteorology,
Science of fickle clouds, ferocious winds.

The day you turned twenty-six fighter planes cut a storm,
Fissured air baring the heart's intricate meshwork

Of want and need—
Springs of cirrus out of which sap and shoot you raised me.

Crossing Chand Bibi Road,
Named after the princess who rode with hawks,

Slept with a gold sword under her pillow,
Raced on polo fields,

You saw a man lift a child, her chest burnt with oil,
Her small thighs bruised.

He bore her through latticed hallways
Into Lady Dufferin's hospital.

How could you pierce the acumen of empire,
Mesh of deception through which soldiers crawled,

Trees slashed with petrol,
Grille work of light in a partitioned land?

When you turned away,
Your blue black hair was crowned with smoke—

You knelt on a stone. On your bent head
The monsoons poured.

Birthplace with Buried Stones

I

In the absence of reliable ghosts I made aria,
Coughing into emptiness, and it came

A west wind from the plains with its arbitrary arsenal:
Torn sails from the Ganga river,

Bits of spurned silk,
Strips of jute to be fashioned into lines,

What words stake—sentence and make-believe,
A lyric summoning.

II

I came into this world in an Allahabad hospital,
Close to a smelly cow pasture.

I was brought to a barracks, with white walls
And corrugated tin roof,

Beside a civil aviation training center.
In World War II officers were docketed there.

I heard the twang of propellers,
Jets pumping hot whorls of air,

Heaven bent,
Blessing my first home.

III

In an open doorway, in half darkness
I see a young woman standing.

Her breasts are swollen with milk.
She is transfixed, staring at a man,

His hair gleaming with sweat,
Trousers rolled up

Stepping off his bicycle,
Mustard bloom catches in his shirt.

I do not know what she says to him,
Or he to her, all that is utterly beyond me.

Their infant once a clot of blood
Is spectral still.

Behind this family are vessels of brass
Dotted with saffron,

The trunk of a mango tree chopped into bits,
Ready to be burnt at the household fire.

IV

Through the portals of that larger chaos,
What we can scarcely conceive of in our minds—

We'd rather think of starry nights with biting flames
Trapped inside tree trunks, a wellspring of desire

Igniting men and gods,
A lava storm where butterflies dance—

Comes bloodletting at the borders,
Severed tongues, riots in the capital,

The unspeakable hurt of history:
So the river Ganga pours into the sea.

V

In aftermath—the elements of vocal awakening:
Crud, spittle, snot, menstrual blistering,

Also infant steps, a child's hunger, a woman's rage
At the entrance to a kitchen,

Her hands picking up vegetable shavings, chicken bones,
Gold tossed from an ancestral keep.

All this flows into me as mottled memory,
Mixed with syllables of sweat, gashed syntax,

Strands of burst bone in river sand,
Beside the buried stones of Sarasvati Koop—

Well of mystic sky-water where swans
Dip their throats and come out dreaming.

QUESTION TIME

I remember the scarred spine
Of mountains the moon slips through,

Fox fire in a stump, bushes red with blisters,
Her question, a woman in a sweatshirt,

Hand raised in a crowded room—
What use is poetry?

Above us, lights flickered,
Something wrong with the wiring.

I turned and saw the moon whirl in water,
The Rockies struck with a mauve light,

Sea creatures cut into sky foliage.
In the shadow of a shrub once you and I

Brushed lips and thighs,
Dreamt of a past that frees its prisoners.

Standing apart I looked at her and said—
We have poetry

So we do not die of history.
I had no idea what I meant.

Afterwards, Your Loneliness

There was not so much as a handful of dust which was not red with the blood of men whose bodies were like the rose.

—MIRZA GHALIB, DELHI, 1857

I

You were holed up in the cold.
No oil to light the lamps, even mice started shivering.
You had to sell your clothes, the camel hair robe,

Woolen kurta knit with finest lamb's wool, Turkish cap, all of it,
Down to the cotton coverings she stitched for your bed,
All this to get a few morsels of food

For yourself and that mad brother
Who tore cotton, silk, off his own flesh
And started scratching—unbearable itch, he had, poor Yusuf.

At night you waited for a lightning flash
So you could put out your hands,
Touch paper, ink.

The lane where you lived was shut with stones,
Big stones to keep out the Brits,
Shoved against the mouth of the gully.

Roses crumpled, petals sucked into crevices of rock,
Kikar trees on the ridge held out a crown of thorns.
You stumbled out, stick in hand, from Kashmiri Gate.

II

In the blood spotted alleyway and on the causeway,
Clouds cling to a spittoon of fire.
People gather in starlight and smoke,

Dragonflies shimmer on burnt metal.
Threads of light stitch us
Into other selves we long to be—ruinous metamorphosis.

III

Why does no one come? You are hard of hearing.
Lights flicker, the mirror darkens.
The postal system is in chaos:

A letter sent to Victoria—Diamond of the Sky, Maker of Kings—
Concerning your pension,
Who knows if she ever got it?

Be near me, you cry,
As dung spills into your lane.
Were you speaking to the angels who live in your head?

There is one world of mud, another of spirit.

Mirza Ghalib
Show us where the horizon goes,
Where sight must cease.

Your loneliness makes fiery footprints in the soil,
Stars throw down their spears.
Spirit signs come closer and closer.

Plot of Tiger Lilies

When Mirza Ghalib saw a bathhouse keeper
Burnt by passion,
A brown man with bits of dirt

On his face and thighs,
He knew that the sun had to be sucked
Into the leaf of his manuscript—

So that in unremitting light
The human stain would pour straight into soil
And blunt rock.

I am dying into my own life—he wrote—
There is no help for this.
Only music without words.

My body is growing old
And so I need to remember
This body, this flesh.

*

A child who befriends stones,
Searching out ants for company,
Letting them crawl on her flesh—

Putting clear things together
So they would make a cacophony
Ruled by a richer harmonic

That the poet sought, dreaming
A dark corona around their faces
As they stood still in the garden.

*

Picture the child
Carrying around the wound
That no one else could see,

Fearing it would slop blood
Over the stiff sheets on the line,
In a garden planted with tiger lilies,

Water in a black well,
The gleaming pot of hair
On the cowherd's thighs.

*

Music originally for voices
Now for the sun—
A poet making music with no words.

I think of the child I once was.
She saw nakedness,
And was terribly moved. How old was I?

Lost Garden

I

A space without history—
At the rim of the pond grandmother loosens her sari,
Her skin glistens, utterly bare. No one remembers this.

Lotus petals flicker under the axle tree.
Tree of heaven they call it in the family.
By its roots grandfather made a fire, tossed in her poems,

Poor things, penned in black ink.
She had folded them into finicky squares,
Buried them in her jewel case with ravenous rubies,

Slow sift of sapphire,
Poems of no climate
Words halting, quick with longing

For a man whose name no one knew.
Two whole months she took to her bed
Her hands bent under her, refusing what food she could.

One night she stumbled out,
Ran her fingers over scorched bark—
Alstonia scholaris—what was left of his body

Imagined reliquary,
Blushing like koi
Fed from her own hand.

II

Syntax surrenders
To an axe biting into wood,
And hearing small shocks from my past

I know it's all over—
The years of childhood,
The Innocence of Before and After,

Seasons of rain, fragrance of burnt blossoms
And under the axle tree, stars
Musk scented, acutely unreal.

In the shadow of that tree
Mirza Ghalib comes to me,
Lamb's wool cap askew, flecked with blood—

I tried to wash it in your grandmother's pond, he said.
I saw it was crowned
With speckled eggs.

He knelt on the ground where a tree once stood—
I can see through this hole to the island city
Where you've gone to live,

In the glory of the Beloved all borders vanish.
I saw her then in moonlight,
A girl whose breath was like my own.

Her wrists were stumps.
Her black hair blew into resurrection waves,
She could not comb it back.

She was grandmother
And she was me,
And she skipped up the diamond stairs into the sky.

III

In glowing heat, in blessed synchrony
I saw what Ghalib saw—
Houses with their eyes plucked out,

Books knifed, goblets shattered
Townspeople, some in soiled dhotis,
Twirling from the lampposts.

O lilies he wrote on his sleeve,
Your mouths are filled with dust.
Love draws us down into history.

Men on horseback carrying incense and myrrh,
All the way from Mecca to Manhattan,
Dream of a garden where a poet sips wine

From the crook of your elbow—
O girl with moonlit hair whose wrists are stumps!
Then whispering so I had to stoop to hear:

Beloved my body is scarred with age
Fit for burial,
While yours gleams

Rainbow colored.
In the rain washed trees
There is nothing to see but nakedness.

Stump Work

I

Sunlight sets up a green-gold glass
On the pond in the poor man's park,
A blackness of Narcissus in the swan's beak.
Out of cinders and rooting chemicals
A blue flower shoots—a city clambers up.
She flows, *robbed and tore.*
Who called her, who named her love?
Who swung out knees and fists?
In the grove where she stumbled,
Stones river. She soldiers on
A woman bruised and born.
Something hurtles in the sky,
A form of fire.
On stippled water, swans drink in the light.

II

The swans are darkening their feathers with kohl,
They want to be beautiful.
A blind head goes where a beak can't.
On the mountain, larks flit into nothingness—
Brightness in water for a god rushing through.
A blessing haunts a soldier's lips,
A man drags his shadow upstream,
A prisoner whirls on a water board,
Blotches of snot, shards of cartilage.
Under raised wings, the body's broken grove.
Once in the valley of Swat
A child herded goats, raced his golden kite.
Now trees shift their vernacular
Into a lost script, throats burst in flight.

III

The ladder was made of salt, it started to crumble.
I looked for you in the garden.
The flowers had drunk up all the water
Lilies—shrimps of sorrow, jasmine
The color of gems harvested from the hill
Where the house stood, just a single tree to shelter it.
Outside the window, the yard where the child lay,
Her face exposed, earthworms jubilant.
Already it was tomorrow, brutal drums,
Red harmonium of war, all things smoldering,
The ragged assonance of longing turning them
Wholly other, the dragonfly leaping from the corpse,
The corpse opening its eyes
To the astonished lapis of the sky.

IV

You loaded me into the wind,
As if I were a dragonfly, blowing softly.
Under the slurry wall swallows were mating.
My thighs were bruised.
Threads of silt packed into vesicles,
A man's arm, a boy's kneecap,
A girl's milk tooth, a slip of silk curling.
On Lispenard Street I heard wings beat,
A man and woman in love's flood—
Something in those eyes, a startled music.
On lowly ground, I knelt,
A mute thing, seeing a slit of blood.
Inside the ruined columbarium
Shot veins sing.

Star Drift

I sit by the window staring at the sky,
On the sidewalk, a mess of reddish leaves.
Three girls strut by,
Heels sharp as bird beaks,
Hair piled onto delicate necks; the tallest sports
A tank top marked with stars and Milky Way.

When Sarpedon began to bleed
Twin gods descended—
Thanatos and his brother whose name is Sleep.
They gathered up leaves
From the rim of the battlefield,
Touched them to the dying man's eyes.

Who can outlive the chaos of the world?
The leaves of Hypnos
Pressed to a warrior's eyes
Begin to smoke, then burn.
We read in the *Iliad* that Sarpedon
Was borne into the sky by the twins.

Stars drift to the ground where corpses lie.
Three girls whispering secrets
Pass by Tip-Top Pharmacy.
They do not stop (they are not in search of a cure).
They flutter through the doorway of a nail salon,
Songbirds smeared with light.

Graduation 1949

I walk into the street and it comes to me . . .
—ROY DeCARAVA

She is at the brink of something she cannot see.
Out of the shadows comes the Chevrolet Bel Air—Style Star of an All Star Line

And it's large and painted red though in the photo soft gray
And seems to be made of lead. Where will it take her?

Her skirts are ringed with dirt.
They rest on asphalt with trash blown over, fit entry to the underworld.

Her dress was bought for more money than she had—
Rustling organza, flickering tulle, pouf sleeves

Pouring skirts, bodice pinched under tight breasts,
Elbows hooked into white gloves.

What is tiny looms large, shadows start to sing.
Out of the shadows comes the Chevrolet Bel Air.

Step away child from that Chevrolet car.
What will your mother do without you?

You are one of three sisters, this I know, ,
The middle one who cried herself to sleep

Turning plain wool over and over in bare hands,
Stroking the blue cotton dress in grandmother's closet—Harlem 1949.

You inherit a realm of shivering bottle caps,
Boys playing stickball, girls at fountains where mad dogs bark.

Rose hips glisten in a wintry park,
A blind piano player shuffles into a jazz bar,

Another wipes spit from his lips with a bit of silk,
Hoists a trumpet fit to blast music for a heavenly host.

Girl child in the too much shining dress,
You drift into an empty lot on the upper reaches of Lexington.

Out of a heap of newsprint, bits and pieces of filth,
Springs the many headed narcissus, glistening flower with its hundred roots.

You turn in surprise,
Lifting your skirts so the dirt will not hurt the hems.

We catch your face mirrored in a scent
No mother can save you from or father rock you free—O Persephone.

Reading Imru' al-Qays on the Subway

Every spirit builds itself a house.
—EMERSON

I

Clothing heaped on the uneven stones of the sidewalk
A ripped shirt, one sleeve blue another green,

One cut up and stuffed within the other—
How else to make a garment latch over itself like this?

Useful to someone struggling to stay warm,
Discarded later at the mouth of the subway

(Before winter breaks, all things are possible).
Against the stained wall by the pizza shop,

Gazelle spoors the color of peppercorns,
Also a plastic cup I step over

Not knowing quite where I am, or why
I must make my way through the entrails of a city.

I need to forget racks of jagged speed,
Metal teeth sprung from the escalator, zone of punctual alarm.

Stop! Is how the Arabic poem began, the one
I murmur over and over again in plain translation.

Is that any way to start a poem, one might ask.
Only if it veers into greatness which the *Mu'allaqa* does.

Some say the poem was inscribed in gold on fine Egyptian linen,
Draped on the Black Stone—heaven dropped.

II

The pizza shop, soon to disappear, is functional still,
The customers have their backs to me, one turns,

He is chewing an unburnt cigarette.
Latched between a tall granite building and another pale

And stuccoed, blue scoops itself free,
Glinting as a wristwatch might.

Indigo wings spill, ring in effortless harmony,
Vanishing into clouds that darken, drift

In an evanescence words can barely hint at—
A rhythm reaching the woman on the fourth floor.

She hears music in her head.
Does it come from the trumpet player on the street below

One foot poised on a pile of new lumber?
I see trees of green . . . red roses too . . .

Picking up her skirt, she runs the long steps to the library
And finds in the half dark everything emblazoned,

Walls, video screens,
Unbearable clarity of an alphabet she will never read.

Several floors above her, a man in shirt sleeves walks fast,
Head bent, making for a glass door.

Its mirror startles him—he halts.
Are those gazelles, pale creatures with huge polished eyes

That leapt in the sands between al-Dakhul and Hawmal?
He hears the ambulance by the Empire State

Glimpses a torn shirt tossed in a steep wind—
If my actions grieve you, let us separate your clothes from mine.

III

Surface air stretches, mixing into unseen filaments
Gilding the windowpane,

The golden trumpet in a poor man's hands,
Reflected in the waters on Resurrection Day.

Branches of air above the oasis so loved by Imru' al-Qays
In time's slow burn, bear necklaces of rain.

A long cord of traffic halts.
Flags above the stone building billow into wings.

Crossing the street, I loosen my old raincoat,
Slip into the radiant wet of things.

On Indian Road

I

I have come drawn to water,
Rooks in trees preparing for winter
A glazed horseshoe dropped a century ago,

Bits of arrowhead
From those who lived on this land,
Who thought the sun and moon beloved companions.

We were young,
Hair the color of crow feathers,
Mine spilling down, yours spiking skyward.

You had a shawl
Flung over your shoulders.
About you, the glamor of the very young poet.

We stood at a stall sipping tea.
A lorry painted with a four-armed goddess scratched to a halt.
The driver waved at us, strolled into the bushes.

Who is the greatest singer in the world?
Breathless, you picked up your own question—
Begum Akhtar. Who else? You must love her too.

My heart is given, I replied, to M. S. Subbulakshmi.
I will not take it back.
On the road where we stood it started to rain,

Under the neem roots
Earthworms wriggled.
I heard a supernal, fleshly music.

II

Shahid—the movie theater where they showed *Fire*
Is burnt, rexine seats and all.
At the rim of Dal Lake, boats smolder.

In your valley I see a girl, her feet so very clean,
Washed in a slipstream.
Her face pale, her kurta jonquil colored

March birth flower,
For the month she died.
On her left breast, the marks of barbed wire.

You said you were at the last ghat of the world,
What did you mean?
A heron, feathers bloodshot, swims to the horizon.

Love is its own compulsion—
In dreams you become a black god,
Our splintered geographies of desire

Sucked into meteors,
Flaming round your head.
Now I hear your voice in the cherry trees

In the thud of lost arrowheads,
In the resolute clip-clop of horses,
Manes blown into the sun.

You stroll through clouds: beside you chinars float,
Four of them, making a secret island.
By me, small boats rock, hulls singing.

(In memory of Agha Shahid Ali, 1949–2001)

Elegy

In your nostrils, the scent of paddy,
Bittersweet of whisky, flash of chili

On a branch of the tree of heaven,
Your jute bag, swinging.

We sat together near the tree,
You had a book of pictures

Sunlight fell
On *Wheatfield with Crows* dazzling me.

Those birds are question marks
Coming, or fleeing?

The middle path,
In between the other two

It flows through wild wheat and golden,
Part of the ground, part of us.

In the town where you were born,
A doe leaps over thorns.

A woman pulls a saffron thread out of torn cloth,
Uses it to mend a child's skirt.

We must listen to each other,
How else shall we live?

Your voice, filled with the musk
Of green leaves

Breaking my heart—
Already night becomes you.

(In memory of Ramu Gandhi, 1937–2007)

STONE BRIDGE

I went walking over a cold stone bridge
Beside the Fondamenta degli Incurabili.
A child went ahead with a cat on a leash,
An old man traipsed behind, a fedora on his head,
The clouds were pink with giggling cherubs.
I saw you at the window of a second-floor room
Filled with sickness no one understood,
Your hair brushed back and your elbow taut
Against the wall: the Russian plains hung in a print
Gathering darkness and the snows of Siberia
Boiled on the gas stove, in a simple pot you bought
In Rialto market—and everywhere the sounds
Of the alphabet grating against fine paper,
The whispers of those forced against their will,
Cold fists of infants on death's hill.

(In memory of Joseph Brodsky, 1940–1996)

SNOW

At the pitch heart of winter my parents appear
Dressed in thin cotton, holding hands.
He's come from a tent reared in the clouds,
And she from a house with a stony courtyard.
In her black cooking pot, goldfish crawl.
Not far from his grave, twin hummingbirds
Fasten nests to the rim of a pond.
Short strokes of water rise up and store
Darkness. They need me now,
See how my parents turn up as it snows,
Blanched petals of the lotus shredded and blown.
They never knew such treasure in their lives:
They reach for it now as it trembles on trees.

Sita's Abduction with Shadow Puppets

I

At midnight as the conch shell blew
(Invisible hands held it aloft)

Tugged by two lads, the curtain fell,
The upper portion misty white where heavens start.

Underneath stitched on tight, nether quarters,
Hell and all that, what even the king's horsemen fear—

Night heaped on painted darkness as the sea pours,
Crabs, turtles, swordfish, each with its delicate shell or snout:

An ancient tale redacted in the stiffness of deer's skin,
Tiny eyes pierced (using a golden awl).

So lamplight darts, wicks thirsty,
Firing a theater of shadows.

II

How simple it looks: Rama and Sita under a pipal tree,
The garden filled with songbirds, mottled rosebuds, a singing fountain.

But what lies above, below, who can tell?
Go lovely song . . . so the envoi goes.

Dashed from midair, parrots dive,
Eight men summoned from the paddy fields,

Cymbals ring, trees quiver.
Ten-headed Ravana shoves her into a net.

His chariot bumps over the waves, a riderless horse clops behind.
In *Kampan Ramayana*

The king and his crew catch Ravana,
Slit his ten throats with a golden sword, rescue Sita—

Her arms were lashed with wet lotus stalks,
Her cheeks were smeared with rouge.

III

Drumbeats call a halt.
Before a triumphal return, before the ocean crossing,

The screen must fall.
Stitched cloth (both the heaven and hell of it) is dropped into boiling water.

Two lads bob behind a bush to take a leak,
One man lays down his gleaming drum, another his flute.

Something flutters free, uncoils its simmering length.
A war hoisted by her beauty, a desperate undoing,

Ends as wars rarely do—in tumultuous healing.
A conch shell whistles,

A hoarse voice keens a shadow tale
Marking mortality,

Sempiternal emptiness,
What we so rarely reach, harmonic wind and water

Fragments poured into place.
The sun serene over ordinary earth:

And what she cried out in the ruined garden of her mind
Becomes part of the barbarous hold of things

An exquisite soundless scream let loose to warm graves,
Encircling air, an invisible audience waiting.

Red Boat

A little red boat
      In Cape Cod Bay,
A lightness at its core
      As the wind blows.
Where does it go
      When night comes?
No one knows.

ACKNOWLEDGMENTS

I am grateful to the editors of the journals where these poems first appeared:

Black Renaissance/Renaissance Noire: "In the Garden of Freemasons,"
   "Question Time," "Reading Imru' al-Qays on the Subway" (under the
   title "Resurrection Day"), "Water Crossing" (under the title "Living in
   the World")
Callaloo: "Graduation 1949"
Guernica: "Nocturne"
Harvard Review: "Experimental Geography," "Morning Ritual"
The Hindu Literary Review: "Mamilla Cemetery"
Indiana Review: "Snow"
The Kenyon Review: "Cobblestones and Heels"
KR Online: "Garden in Nazareth"
Literary Imagination: Sonnets II, III of "Stump Work" (under the titles "Jihad"
   and "Exequy")
The Literary Review: "Damage." In a slightly different form, this poem cycle
   appeared in the online literary magazine *Almost Island.*
The Little Magazine: "Sita's Abduction with Shadow Puppets"
The Massachusetts Review: "Nocturnal with Ghostly Landscape on St. Lucy's
   Day," "On Indian Road"
Meridians: "Lost Garden" (under the title "The Garden"). This poem also
   appears in *Writing Love: An Anthology of Indian-English Poetry,* ed. Ashmi
   Ahluwalia (New Delhi: Rupa, 2010).
The New Yorker: "Lady Dufferin's Terrace"
Norman Mailer Writers Colony Blog (July 30, 2011): "Red Boat"
Painted Bride Quarterly: "Stone Bridge," Sonnet IV of "Stump Work" (under
   the title "Wind Song")
phati'tude Literary Magazine: Sonnet I of "Stump Work" (under the title
   "Traces")
Ploughshares: "Birthplace with Buried Stones"
Postcolonial Text: "Elegy," "Indian Hospice," "Teatro Olimpico"
Prairie Schooner: "For My Father, Karachi 1947," "Summer Splendor." These
   two poems received the Glenna Luschei Prairie Schooner Award.

The Threepenny Review: "Migrant Memory"

TriQuarterly: "Plot of Tiger Lilies" (under the title "In the Garden of Tiger Lilies")

TriQuarterly Online: "Impossible Grace," "Red Bird"

Washington Square Review: "Landscape with Kurinji Flowers"

Weber: The Contemporary West: "Afterwards, Your Loneliness," "Boy from Rum"

World Literature Today: "June Air," "Star Drift" (under the title "Sitting in Starbucks")

WSQ: "Mother, Windblown"

*

These poems in the opening section—"Morning Ritual," "Lychees," "Red Bird," "Bryant Park," "Near Sendai," "Bamboo," "Suite 19, Viceregal Lodge," "Landscape with Ghost," "Lady Dufferin's Terrace"—are also published as a limited-edition chapbook, *Shimla: A Poem Cycle* (New York: Glenn Horowitz Bookseller, 2012). My thanks to Glenn Horowitz.

"Teatro Olimpico," "Nocturne," "Cobblestones and Heels," "Indian Hospice," "Garden in Nazareth," "Impossible Grace," and "Mamilla Cemetery" appear in the limited-edition chapbook *Impossible Grace: Jerusalem Poems* (Jerusalem: Centre for Jerusalem Studies, Al-Quds University, 2012). My thanks to Huda Imam.

The poem "Impossible Grace" was set to music by Stefan Heckel (winner of the Al Quds Music Award) and sung by baritone Christian Oldenburg, Hind el Husseini College, in Jerusalem on October 7, 2012. My thanks to Petra Klose.

*

My special gratitude to the John Simon Guggenheim Foundation for a Fellowship in Poetry allowing me the time and space for composition. I could not have done it without the support. Thanks to the Camargo Foundation for three sun-filled months in Cassis, on the Mediterranean; to Hunter

College for giving me the time to travel and write; to Peter de Souza of the Indian Institute of Advanced Study in Shimla, for inviting me as a visiting professor—it was in the Himalayas that I was able to imagine other lives from the past, ghosts that still haunt us. And how can I forget Sari Nusseibeh, whom I met at the Institute in Shimla. He sensed my longing to see Jerusalem again—I had last been there as a child—and with great kindness he invited me to come as Poet-in-Residence to Al Quds University. It was there, almost unknown to me, that the heart of this book started to take shape. My thanks to the Fulbright Foundation for a Senior Specialist Award which allowed me a month in residence at Ca' Foscari, University of Venice—I sat by the Zattere and dared to imagine a whole book. I carried this manuscript with me as I travelled, and it grew in bits and pieces, on scraps of paper, in notebooks, sometimes on a laptop, and of course in the rhythms of memory—I often compose as I walk. At the Norman Mailer Center and Writers Colony at the edge of the shimmering waters of Cape Cod Bay I was able to complete poems begun in the Himalayas and write new poems. At the Vermont Studio Center I was able to complete "Cantata for a Riderless Horse."

*

One writes in loneliness, that seems to be the way. But I could not imagine completing this work without friends who heard the music in these poems, read the text with care, offered thoughts: Kimiko Hahn, Rosanna Warren, Lila Cecil, Wallis Wilde Menozzi, Ronaldo Wilson, Leah Souffrant. My thanks to Marco Fazzini and Andrea Sirotti for translations into Italian, and to Huda Imam and Zahra Rashidi for translations into Arabic.

*

My gratitude to my family for being here: David, above all, who has lived through the writing of this book; Adam and Svati, growing in beauty and light in a time of turbulence; my mother and my sisters Anna and Elsa, our ever-present kinship drawing strength from the dark waters that separate us; closer at hand, my friend Gauri Viswanathan and my cousin Verghis Koshi.

"Morning Ritual" and other poems (Shimla cycle)
For a month in the summer of 2010 I lived in Shimla, in the old Viceregal
Lodge. I had a suite of rooms with a terrace that looked out onto the
Himalayas. I carried a copy of Bashō with me; I felt his lines might help me
in my journey. Sometimes I would sit on the terrace and write, sometimes in
the shadow of a pipal tree. Images came to me as I walked on the twisting
paths. Other places are also evoked in this cycle of poems: the Lodi Gardens
in Delhi, where I used to live; Bryant Park, a place I love in New York City;
Sendai in Japan, which I could only imagine.

*

"Lady Dufferin Writes to Her Mother"
This poem happened after reading Lady Dufferin's memoir, *Our Viceregal
Life in India, Selections from My Journal, 1884–1888,* by the Marchioness of
Dufferin and Ava (London: Murray, 1889), 2 vols.

*

"Landscape with Kurinji Flowers"
The *kurinji* is a rare mauve-blue flower that is found only in the hills of
southern India. Evoked in love poetry of the classical Tamil anthologies, it
blossoms every twelve years. My poem was composed in the aftermath of the
attacks on Bombay in November 2008.

*

"Mother, Windblown"
In the year 1230, Iltutmish completed work on a victory tower, the Qutb
Minar in Delhi; the Jardin des Vestiges, once part of an ancient Phoenician
settlement, is in Marseille. I visited both (scenes of migratory civilizations)
during a long journey.

*

"Boy from Rum"
The painting is from a leaf of a dispersed manuscript of the *Khamsa* of

Amir Khusrau Dihlavi. The poet (Amir Khusrau, 1253–1325) was gifted as a musician.

*

"Teatro Olimpico"
I composed this poem in Italy, after a visit to Venice. Somehow the separation wall came into it. I had the poem with me and read it out a week later, April 7, 2011, at the Al Midani theater, Haifa, during a memorial for Juliano Mer-Khamis. My thanks to Khaled Furani for taking me to Haifa.

*

"Nocturne"
The lines in italics come from Mahmoud Darwish, *Mural,* trans. Rema Hammami and John Berger (London: Verso, 2009).

*

"Mamilla Cemetery"
In April 2011, I visited Mamilla Cemetery. This ancient place of Muslim burial was being torn apart by the Israeli authorities in order to build a Museum of Tolerance. I am grateful to Huda Imam and Jamal Nusseibeh for taking me there.

*

"Water Crossing"
Composed in Cassis, September 29–October 9, 2008. Under the title "Living in the World" it first saw the light of day in fall 2009 in French translation by Claire Malraux: "Vivre dans ce monde," "*Siècle 21* (Paris). The last two lines of this poem come from Virgil's Eclogue IX in David Ferry's translation, *The Eclogues of Virgil* (New York: Farrar, Straus & Giroux, 1999), 71.

*

"Afterwards, Your Loneliness"
In his memoir *Dastanbuy* Mirza Ghalib speaks of what he went through in the aftermath of the 1857 revolt. He was living in Delhi when the British, in retaliation, destroyed much of the city. The English text I used is Mirza Ghalib,

Dastanbuy, trans. Khwaja Ahmad Faruqi (New York: Asia Publishing House, 1970). I am grateful to David for reading an earlier version, and to Professor C. M. Naim for guidance.

*

"Stump Work"
The title alludes to a seventeenth-century form of raised embroidery, of elaborate design, often stuffed with fabric or hair. I composed this sonnet cycle in conversation with John Donne's poetry. I was fortunate to see the Westmoreland Manuscript in the Berg Collection at the New York Public Library, vellum fair copy, the cover alabaster colored, so light falls through.

The first poem was evoked by "Show Me Dear Christ" (no. 18), the second by "Batter My Heart" (no. 14), and the third by "Thou Hast Made Me" (no. 1). The last poem came as an aftermath. After seeing the manuscript, I printed out each Donne poem from the Web, pasted it into my notebook, and composed each line of my poem in between Donne's lines, a species of poetic hatching if you will. I am grateful to Isaac Gewirtz, curator of the Berg Collection, for showing me the manuscript.

*

"Graduation 1949"
The poem was inspired by a photograph by Roy DeCarava of the same name. I read "Graduation 1949" at the memorial and celebration for Roy DeCarava held in the Great Hall at Cooper Union, New York City, May 10, 2010. My thanks to Sherry Turner DeCarava for inviting me.

*

"Reading Imru' al-Qays on the Subway"
"I see trees of green . . ." comes from the lyrics of Louis Armstrong's "What a Wonderful World." "If my actions grieve you . . ." comes from Imru' al-Qays, *Mu'allaqa*, trans. Basima Bezirgan and Elizabeth Fernea, in Jacques Berque, *Cultural Expression in Arab Society Today* (Austin: University of Texas Press, 1978), 111.